W9-BIC-073

MY HIDDEN CHIMP

BY PROF STEVE PETERS

Helping children to understand and manage their emotions, thinking and behaviour with **TEN** helpful habits

MY HIDDEN CHIMP

BY PROF STEVE PETERS

Graphic storytelling by Jeff Battista

A STUDIO PRESS BOOK
First published in the UK in 2018 by Studio Press,
an imprint of Bonnier Books UK,
4th Floor, Victoria House, Bloomsbury Square, London WC1B 4DA
Owned by Bonnier Books,
Sveavägen 56, Stockholm, Sweden

www.bonnierbooks.co.uk

Text © Mindfield Media Limited 2018
Illustrations © Jeff Battista 2018

Prof Steve Peters has asserted his moral right to be
identified as the author of this Work in accordance with
the Copyright, Designs and Patents Act 1988.

14 16 18 20 19 17 15 13

All rights reserved.
ISBN 978-1-78741-371-9 (Paperback)
ISBN 978-1-78741-435-8 (eBook)

FSC
www.fsc.org

MIX
Paper from
responsible sources
FSC® C104723

Written by Prof Steve Peters
Designed by Jeff Battista

A CIP catalogue for this book is available from the British Library
Printed and bound in China

An introduction

After writing **The Chimp Paradox** I received many requests for a simplified version that could be used by children, either alone or with the support of an adult. This book is written to introduce children to some basic neuroscience of the mind using the Chimp model with some applications of this.

As many children learn habits during childhood that are often carried into adult life, I have written this book based on habit formation. I hope it will help young children to develop constructive and healthy habits for life.

Parents, teachers and carers have discussed ideas with me to determine the ten habits that they felt would be helpful for children to acquire.

The book explores how we think and function but everyone is unique. The book offers suggestions for going forward but it is very important that the reader decides what works best for them and their child. The book is not a recipe for improved quality of life. It is about reflecting and developing desirable habits.

I would like to sincerely thank the following people:

Dr Catherine Keep, Consultant Child and Adolescent Psychiatrist, and Dr Hazel Harrison, Clinical Psychologist, for their guidance and support during the writing of the book.

Jeff Battista for the vast amount of time spent producing the graphics and for input into the work.

Kim Blakey for illustrative support in developing the child characters.

My team of readers, who patiently gave comments and suggestions, that were invaluable: Hazel Barker, Dr Sarah Caddy, Andy Varns, Beverley Nesbitt and Tim Buckle.

Thanks to many others who also gave input.

There is
something
hiding that
you should
know about!

Here are some new friends who will help you to find what is hiding.

But first...something is puzzling them.

This book will help solve the puzzle and find what is hiding!

It is best to read this book with an adult and talk about each page as you go along.

But you can read the book on your own if you want to.

It will explain about your feelings and your thinking.

It can help you to feel happier, stop worrying and behave better!

So let's begin...

Do you ever wonder why you do things that you DON'T want to do?

Let's look at some things we all seem to do.

Telling lies:

Have you ever told lies?

It wasn't me. It was someone else who did it!

Tasia didn't really want to lie.

Being mean:

Have you ever been nasty to your brother, sister or friend?

Go away. You're not my friend anymore.

I am so sad and upset. I didn't do anything wrong.

Beth didn't want to upset Joey by being nasty and hurtful.

What is going on?

Getting scared:

Have you ever been so frightened that you couldn't move because you thought that a monster could be under your bed?

In the daylight it seems silly to have been scared.

Joey didn't want to feel scared.

Getting worried:

Have you ever wondered why you got so worried about something and later thought that you were being a bit silly?

Worry! Worry! Worry! Worry!

I am so worried I feel sick!

LATER

Why was I so worried over nothing?

Carl didn't want to be sick with worry.

Being grumpy or angry:

Does Joey really want to be grumpy or does he want to be happy?

 OR

We all do things we wish we hadn't done.

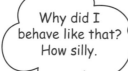

So what is going on?

This book will tell you why we do silly things and how to stop doing them!

This will make some children a lot happier!

Stop! It's time for YOU to help.

Write down **3 things** you've done that you didn't want to do.

1.

2.

3.

It almost seems like there are 2 of you living inside your head!

One of you is happy, not worried and well-behaved.

The other one can be grumpy, worried, silly or naughty.

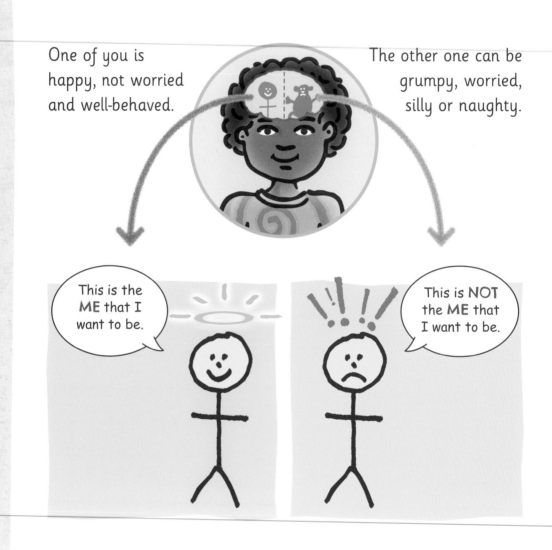

So, if there were 2 of you, which one would you like to be?

 What is going on?

ACTIVITY PAGE

Stop!
It's time for YOU to help.

Write in the boxes below how you want to be, and how you don't want to be.

How do you want to be? Happy, angry, well-behaved, funny, mean...?

What I want to be:	What I don't want to be:

Get ready for a surprise...
there really are 2 of you!

Let's have a **look** at what is inside your head.

A brain

If we look inside someone's head we will see a brain.

It looks like this.

What is going on?

The brain controls your body.

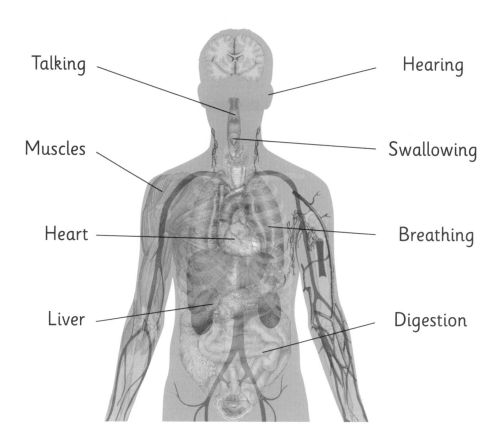

Talking

Muscles

Heart

Liver

Hearing

Swallowing

Breathing

Digestion

Different parts of the brain control different things.

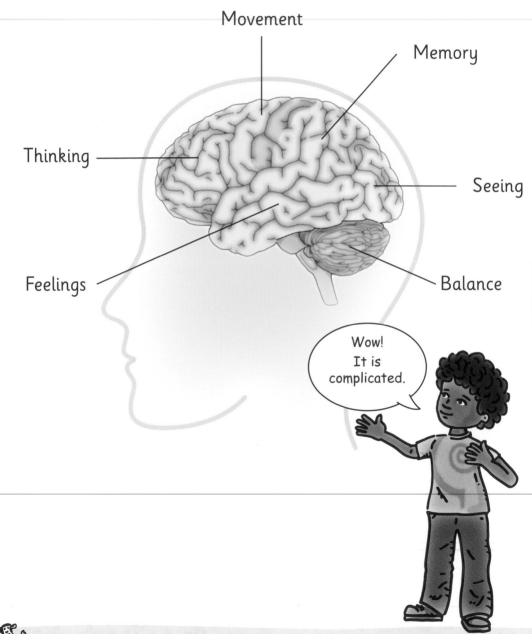

Movement

Memory

Thinking

Seeing

Feelings

Balance

Wow! It is complicated.

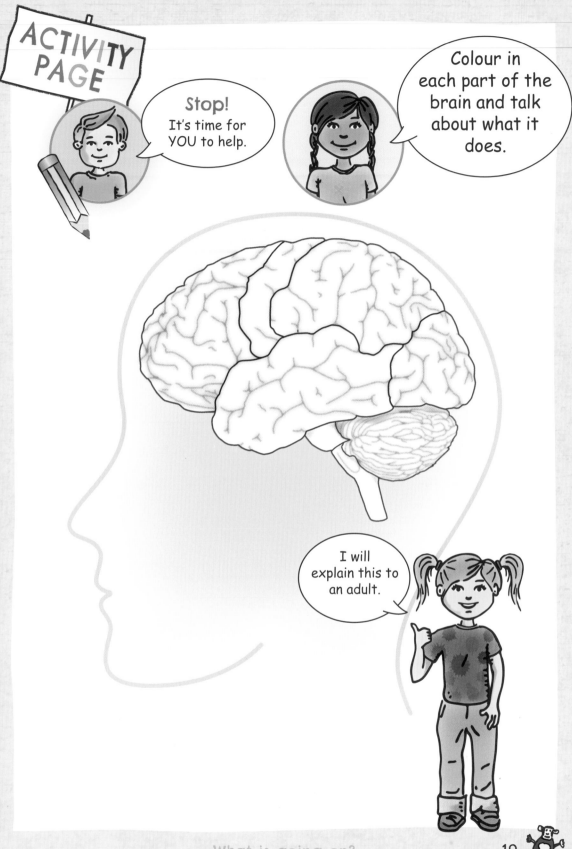

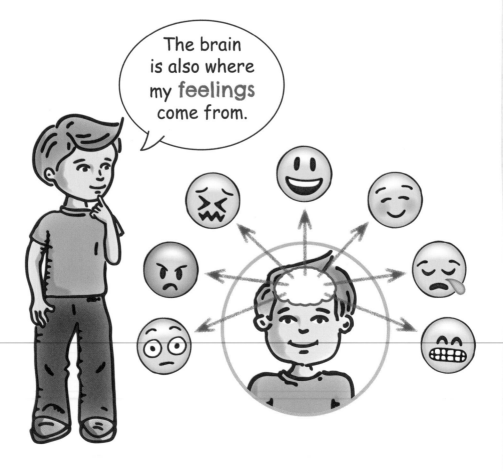

What is going on?

2 parts of our brain are used for thinking.

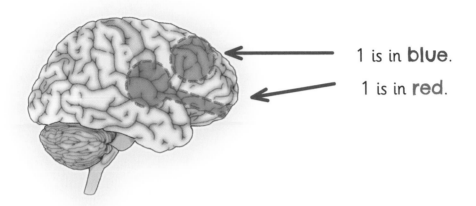

1 is in **blue**.

1 is in **red**.

We can control the **blue brain**.
We can't control the **red brain**!

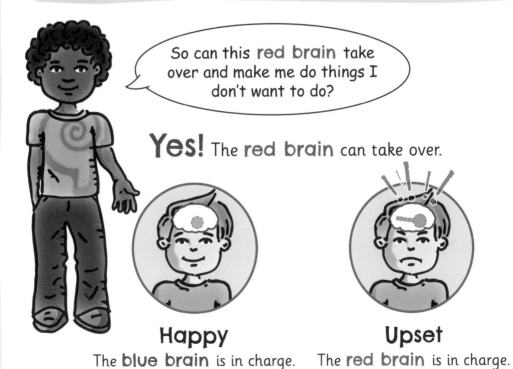

So can this **red brain** take over and make me do things I don't want to do?

Yes! The **red brain** can take over.

Happy
The **blue brain** is in charge.

Upset
The **red brain** is in charge.

Now here comes a shock!

If we look inside the brain of a chimpanzee we see that it also has a **red brain**.

It's the same!

The chimp only has a small **blue brain** that it rarely uses.

So, we might as well call our **red brain** our **"inner Chimp"** brain!

So we have **our brain** and a Chimp brain
living inside our head!

Our brain

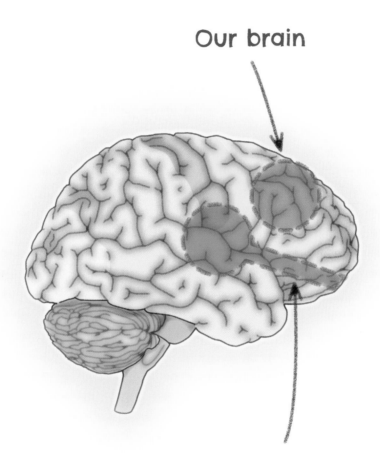

An "inner Chimp" brain

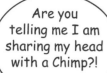 Are you telling me I am sharing my head with a Chimp?!

Not a **REAL** chimpanzee silly.
But it is what **YOU** act like when your "inner Chimp" takes over!

So the Chimp in me is just a word for part of my brain.

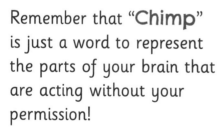

Yes, it is a fun way to know when this part of your brain has taken over.

WOW!
Now we can talk about each other's Chimps.

Remember that "**Chimp**" is just a word to represent the parts of your brain that are acting without your permission!

> **A VERY important point:**
> All the feelings we get are **NORMAL**.
> Some are just not helpful but everybody gets them from their Chimp.

What is going on?

Your brain

You

The Chimp brain

Your Chimp

So there are two of me **thinking!**

 What is going on?

We have made a discovery!

There is a **hidden Chimp** in your head!

I have been hiding here all along and secretly taking charge.

Now you know why you look like a Chimp when you misbehave!

Let's find out more about **YOUR** hidden Chimp... watch carefully for the hidden Chimp in the children's heads!

So what happens when our hidden Chimp takes over?

The Chimp can tell lies.

The hidden Chimp!   Me thinking!

It wasn't me. It was someone else who did it!

I didn't want to say this!

It sounds like a lie, Tasia. How disappointing!

Adult

Oh dear. My Chimp took over. I am in more trouble!

Tasia's Chimp took over!

You

I want to tell the truth.

Your Chimp

I will keep lying and say it wasn't me, even if it makes no sense.

28   What is going on?

Being mean to your brother, sister or friend.

Beth's Chimp took over!

You	Your Chimp

Is there really a monster under your bed?

Joey's Chimp took over because it was frightened.

 What is going on?

Getting anxious and worrying.

Carl's Chimp took over because it was anxious.

Grumpy and angry feelings.

Joey's Chimp took over because something upset it.

ACTIVITY PAGE

Stop!
It's time for YOU to get busy.

Fill in what you think and what your Chimp thinks for each one.

Imagine your Chimp is being really naughty!

	Your thoughts	Chimp thoughts
EXAMPLE **Going to the dentist**	I want to look after my teeth.	I don't care if all my teeth fall out!
Not going to bed		
Playing too many computer games		
Eating too many sweets		

What we have found is that our "2 brains" think very differently.

If we look after our "Chimp" then we can stop it from taking over!

An important point:
You are responsible for stopping your Chimp from taking over!

Let's learn more about your hidden Chimp...

Warning:
Everyone's Chimp is very strong, so you might need to ask for help from an adult to manage it!

What is going on?

ACTIVITY PAGE

Stop!
It's time for YOU to get busy.

Just as everybody is different, our Chimps are different too.

Have a think about what your Chimp is like.

It might be fun to DRAW your Chimp!

My Chimp

There could be lots of **words** to describe **YOUR** Chimp.

Worried

Sad Funny

Mean Bossy

Happy

Playful

Grumpy

Shy Crazy

Naughty

Caring

Laughing

Important point:

As you complete the following pages, you may find that you and your Chimp **share** some of the same words.

I don't always like to share!

I am happy to share.

ACTIVITY PAGE

Stop! It's time for YOU to get busy.

Write the **words** that describe **YOUR** Chimp.

_____
My Chimp's name

Some of the words for my Chimp are fun... Others are **NOT** so nice!

There could be lots of words to describe YOU.

Playful   Busy   Happy

Confident   Calm Funny

Loving   Sensible

Helpful   Considerate

Laughing   Serious

When I take over you might look and feel very differently.

A VERY important point:
Which words describe you if your Chimp doesn't take over?

ACTIVITY PAGE

Stop! It's time for YOU to get busy.

Write the words that describe the best YOU.

The best ME.

[ ] [ ]

[ ] [ ]

[ ] [ ]

[ ] [ ]

[ ] [ ]

_____
My name

It is good being ME when my Chimp isn't taking over!

Can we behave differently when our Chimps are in control?

Yes! You and your Chimp often have very **different ideas**.

You

Your Chimp

I want to go for a walk.

I want to do nothing.

z z z

I like to solve problems.

Talk, talk, talk, talk

Talk, talk, talk, talk

I like to worry about problems.

You can behave very **differently** depending on which brain is in control.

I can think of times when my Chimp has taken over.

Think about things your Chimp has made **YOU** do that you didn't want to do.

I feel like being **grumpy!**

Stop being silly!

You are making me feel bad.

I never did it.

You **liar!** Tell the truth.

Telling lies is getting us into even more trouble!

Aghh! My Chimp is a nightmare – HELP!

Tell me more... especially what I can do to manage my Chimp.

I don't want to be managed!

What is going on?

ACTIVITY PAGE

Stop!
It's time for YOU to get busy.

Draw a picture of a time when **YOUR** Chimp took over.

Don't forget to put thought bubbles to show what your Chimp was thinking.

I don't think my Chimp is always naughty!

Sometimes you and your Chimp can **agree** on what you feel or want to do.

Let's have fun.

That sounds like a good idea.

Let's really enjoy it and share the fun with everyone else.

I didn't win the race.

I am disappointed.

I am really upset and angry and I wanted to win.

What is going on?

Here are more examples of you and your Chimp agreeing.

I would like to go to a party.

I would like to meet my friends.

Sometimes you and your Chimp **disagree** on what you feel or want to do.

My Chimp can really misbehave!

Something is annoying me.

I want to stay calm and sort it out.

I want to show my annoyance.

Deciding on what to eat.

I would like to eat something nice but also healthy.

I want to eat what I like, even if it is not good for me.

What is going on?

My Chimp is so stubborn! Look at these other things.

I can't do what I want to do.

I will have to accept this and do something else.

I will get upset and be cross and grumpy with everyone.

My mood.

I want to be in a good mood and be happy.

I can be moody and won't try to be happy.

When you and your Chimp disagree **YOU** have to make a decision.

Which brain do you want to work with?

You always have a choice!

You or your Chimp?

I need to manage my Chimp.

I will take over if you don't.

Even **adults** have Chimps and you might have seen them in action!

I have told you a BILLION times before. You will NEVER EVER play with ANY toy ever again.

Wow! His Chimp is out and talking silly!

This is a very important point:

We all have a Chimp and we all have to learn to manage it, so that it doesn't take over.

What is going on?

You have a choice.

Which do you think is the best brain to use in the following examples?

Getting ready for bed.

I need to brush my teeth.

I can't be bothered to brush my teeth.

My room is untidy.

I want to tidy up NOW.

I will tidy up later.

Or never!

There is a problem!

"Sometimes I try my best, but my Chimp **takes over** anyway!"

"It starts making me do things that I don't want to do."

"When my Chimp takes over it can make me unhappy."

"I don't care!"

The Chimp can be bossy and also clever.

For example, the Chimp can think of lots of excuses for **NOT** doing the right thing.

"I want to do the right thing."

"I will take over and give you lots of silly excuses."

What is going on?

The Chimp acts quickly.

I understand more about my Chimp now, but why do we have this as part of our brain?

I am really here to look after you and keep you safe and warn you about danger.

But... if I feel scared or nervous I normally overreact.

Sometimes I get so upset that I want to shout, fight and stomp around!

Sometimes I get so scared that I want to run away and hide.

Sometimes I get so nervous that I can't think or move!

OR

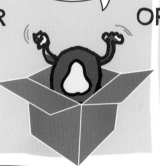

OR

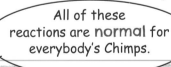

All of these reactions are **normal** for everybody's Chimps.

Important point:

Your Chimp's reaction is **normal** but not always helpful.

That's why we need to help our Chimps and manage them.

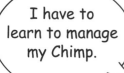
I have to learn to manage my Chimp.

How do we stop our Chimps from speaking and behaving unhelpfully?

I need to learn to look after you, and sometimes I need to put you in a box.

It's probably for the best.

Important point:

YOU can learn how to **choose** which brain you want to work with.

Now we can look at ten habits that might help you to manage your Chimp

... and they will help you to feel happier!

I don't like the sound of this!

1
Smiling

When we are happy we **smile** and everyone can see we are happy.

What happens if we **make** ourselves smile even if we don't want to?

It has been discovered that when you **make** yourself smile it can make you feel **happier**.

Sometimes we just forget to smile!

You smile.

Now your Chimp is happy as well.

Important point:

Smiling, even when you don't feel happy, can actually start making you feel happy!

So how do you learn to smile?

?

How can you **MAKE** yourself smile?

Think about the **good** things you have and this can make you happy and make you smile.

Think about something **funny** that happened or a good time you had.

Smile about it.

Think about people you **like** and smile.

Smiling

Sometimes you are so sad that you don't want to smile.

Smiling

Try and sort out what is making you sad by **telling** someone.

If you are still sad, **take your time** and decide when you want to be happy again.

Decide when your Chimp is really ready to be happy again.

Now help your Chimp to smile!

It's time!

Stop! Over to you to try it for yourself.

PRACTICE PAGE

When I practise smiling, I get **better** at it. Even Fred, my Chimp enjoys this.

Practice 1

When you want to smile try to think of 5 people that you really like and smile for each one of them!

I want to smile for you.

1 2 3 4 5

Practice 2

Think of something that you found funny. Picture it in your mind and see if it brings a smile or even a laugh!

HA! HA! HA!

ACTIVITY PAGE

Stop!
It's time for YOU to get busy.

It really helps me to have a happiness list.

Yes, being happy makes you smile.
Let's make a list of the things that make you happy.

My Happiness List

_____
_____
_____
_____
_____
_____
_____
_____
_____
_____
_____
_____
_____
_____
_____
_____

When you want to be happy do the things on the list!

2

Saying sorry

It makes everyone feel better

Saying sorry

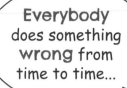 Everybody does something **wrong** from time to time...

 ... but we can say sorry.

Here are some times where saying **sorry** will help.

I screamed!

I had an accident.

I upset someone!

I shouted at someone!

I was being silly.

So what do I do if my Chimp misbehaves?

You can help by saying sorry to the person you might have upset.

Saying sorry also makes **YOU** feel better.

Important point:
It is very wise to learn when to say sorry.

Try to say sorry as soon as you feel bad or realise that you have done something wrong.

Saying sorry as soon as you can is best.

  Saying sorry will make you feel better and it is easy to do.

 I am happier now.

I'm happier as well.

When you have said sorry, you can then try and put things right again.

 What can I do to make things better.

 I would feel better if we can put things right.

Saying sorry helps everyone to feel better and helps people to forgive you. It also helps if you try and put things right after you have said sorry.

Important point: Make sure you really mean it when you say sorry.

Saying sorry

Saying sorry

saying sorry

ACTIVITY PAGE

Stop! It's time for YOU to help.

Can you think of **2 reasons** why saying sorry is the best thing to do?

Can you think of **2 reasons** why your Chimp won't say sorry?

1.

2.

Important point:
Let your Chimp know that you are in charge and that you **WILL** say sorry.

Saying sorry

3

Being kind to someone

How do I learn to be kind to someone, Tasia?

Ask
"Is there something I can do for you?"

I need to ask.

I will help if you ask.

When we help others usually our Chimps become very happy.

Helping others is the right thing to do.

Helping others makes me feel happy as well.

What practical things can we do to be kind to someone?

Helping around the house.

Helping if someone is in trouble.

Oh dear. You have fallen over!

Let me help you up.

Making friends by including them.

Why don't you come and join us?

You have made me very happy.

Being kind to someone

Making pleasant comments about others can help them to feel good.

Letting them know you like them.

Thanking them for something they have given you.

Thanking them for any help they have given you.

Sharing and being kind to your brother, sister or friend.

Being kind to someone

Stop! Over to you to try it for yourself.

1. See **how many** people you can help today.

Can we help you?

That is kind of you to offer.

2. Say something nice to **5 people** today.

Tell them something nice about them.

I like your new trainers.

You look really good.

That is so kind. It makes me feel good.

Being kind to someone

4

Talking about your feelings

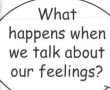 What happens when we talk about our feelings?

Talking about your feelings helps you to **understand** them, especially if you are upset.

It helps me to talk about my feelings and worries.

You can share any feelings with me: sad, happy or excited.

Knowing someone understands how I feel helps me a lot.

I am not always easy to understand.

Important point:
Talking to someone about how you feel is very good for you.

Talking about your feelings

Let's look at my friend Chen who shares his feelings with his Auntie Lin.

Chen is feeling frustrated because things have not been going the way he wanted them to. He is upset.

He talks with his Auntie Lin and tells her what has been happening and how he has been feeling.

Lin listens and Chen feels better because someone has understood how he feels.

Chen thanks his auntie.

Sometimes my Chimp is **super excited** and happy. I like to share the excitement with my friends.

Sharing how excited I feel makes it even better.

My Chimp Banana-head got over excited, so I had to tell her to calm down!

I am so excited I am going to explode.

It's great to be excited but don't get silly!

I will dance instead.

It's great to see Banana-head so excited, but you are right. She needs to calm down.

Important point:

Sometimes your Chimp needs to let out its excitement first before it can listen.

I decided to talk to someone who cares about me.

Talking about your feelings

ACTIVITY PAGE

Stop!
It's time for YOU to get busy.

Draw a picture of something that you want to talk about.

Talk to someone and explain what the picture is about.

5

Asking
for help

What happens when we ask for help?

We can get things done more **quickly**.

Let's ask for help, Hercules.

Stupid computer! I am really angry!

NO! I am going to fix the silly thing myself!

Hmm... I need to take charge.

I can't work out this computer, so I will ask my uncle if he can help.

Does his uncle help?

Asking for help

Asking for help

So I need to ask for help sooner?

Yes, once you realise you **can't** work something out.

I always like to have a try.

Yes, it's good to have a try, but we have to learn when to stop and ask for help.

Important point:

Most people are happy to help you.

Sometimes I am scared to ask for help, but it is silly not to ask.

We can't get this phone to work!

Sometimes things are tricky to work out, so it is sensible to ask for help.

It makes me look stupid!

Once I didn't understand what the teacher was talking about, and needed to ask a question. Hercules said...

... STOP! Your friends are watching and will think you are **stupid**!

My friends didn't understand either but were too scared to ask.

My teacher was really happy when I asked questions... and so were my friends!

ACTIVITY PAGE

Stop! It's time for YOU to help.

Can you think of 3 silly things your Chimp might say to stop you from asking for help?

Can you respond with 3 sensible things, so that your Chimp will ask for help?

1.

2.

3.

A very important point!

Sometimes I really can't manage Mildred, my Chimp, and it makes me feel upset.

Yes, I struggle to manage Fred, he is so strong-minded.

I am glad they haven't thought of asking an adult to help to manage me.

I just had a thought. Why we don't we ask for help?

Yes, we can always ask an adult to help us manage our Chimps...

Arghh... I don't believe it!

I am happy to help you. We can all work together to manage Mildred and Fred.

Asking for help

6

Showing good manners

Pleasing someone else by being polite

Being polite to other people will make you feel good about yourself.

Showing good manners

Showing good manners

 Showing good manners

Showing good manners

PRACTICE PAGE

Stop! Over to you to try it for yourself.

It's time to practise so that you can develop good manners.

Practise saying **"thank you"** to people when they have done something for you or are just nice to you.

I definitely need to practise.

Thank you for what you have done.

More practice!

See how many times in one day that you can say "thank you"... and mean it!

Your teacher, your friend, the bus driver, when getting off the bus, a parent... who else can you think of to say "thank you" to?

Thank you.

Thank you.

Thank you.

Thank you.

7
Trying new things

What happens when we try something new?

You could do outdoor activities. There are **many** groups that do this.

Join a group, or an outdoor activity.

This is a chance to make new friends.

I am scared people won't like me!

Try new and different foods.

We can try healthier foods and get to like new flavours.

Yuck! But if I get used to them I will probably like them.

Try doing something creative or artistic.

Play a new sport.

Trying new things

Look after a pet = Being RESPONSIBLE

Pets take a lot of time and effort.

Take on a challenge

Trying something new can be **fun** and **rewarding**.

Yes, but our Chimps are sometimes not good at this.

Some new things are good, but others I don't want to try.

Trying new things helps us to get better and more confident, Fred.

I can't do this!

That's why we are doing it, Hercules. We can keep going until we get there!

New challenges can push us to get better.

Ha. Your biggest challenge is managing me!

Warning!

Our Chimps can be lazy or fearful and won't let us try new things.

Don't let them spoil the fun!

Sometimes I can't be bothered if it takes effort.

Don't let your Chimp stop you!

Trying new things

My story is about trying new things.

 My Chimp, Mildred, is terrible for not trying new food.

 Tasia, try these new vegetables. They are very high in vitamins.

I don't like them, they look horrible!

You haven't tried them yet!

Sorry, Mum, that was Mildred. I will try them.

What does Tasia say?

Warning!

When trying new things our Chimps often give up too early.

Try new things with friends because Chimps like company.

Stop! It's time for YOU to help.

If your **best** friend said their Chimp was scared to try new things... can you tell me **3 things YOU** would say to their Chimp to help it to have a go?

1.

2.

3.

I really would like some help.

More help needed please!

Think of **3 foods** that your Chimp won't usually eat that are good for you.

1.

2.

3.

You may like to look online for answers!

Trying new things

8

Accepting when "no" really means "no"!

Accepting when "no" really means "no"!

Our Chimps don't usually accept that
"no" means "no".

Accepting when "no" means "no".

Accepting when "no" really means "no"!

It won't help!

What can Beth do?

Finding something else to do can help.

Talking usually helps a lot.

Important point:

Talk to someone but don't let your Chimp keep grumbling and complaining!

How do I learn to accept when "no" really means "no"?

1st STEP

I let Hercules out for a grumble, **BUT** then I tell him to stop!

2nd STEP

I tell Hercules to **ACCEPT** that **NO** means **NO**.
Then I ask him what would be helpful?

We have to accept 'no'. We can't always have what we want.

Let's decide what would be helpful.

Grrr. It would be helpful if he would shut up!

3rd STEP

We decide on a new activity or plan.

Let's do something else.

I was upset, but I accept it...

... we can still have fun doing something else!

Accepting when "no" really means "no"!

Let's see this habit in action!

I am really looking forward to playing with Carl.

You have an appointment at the dentist, Joey, so you can't play.

Oh no! I have to go to the dentist and can't go and play.

NO WAY! I am going to play.

Total frustration!

1st STEP

OK if you need to moan then have a moan, but I will say "STOP" very soon.

Say STOP!

Moan! Moan! Moan! Complain!

Warning:
Tell whoever is near you that you are just letting your Chimp complain!

2nd STEP

Accept.

We must accept that "NO" means "NO". So what else can we do?

It is so annoying! But I will accept "no" and I will calm down.

3rd STEP

Make a new plan.

We can play another day, but now we have to go to the dentist.

I guess it is good to have teeth!

I made plans to play another day.

These were MY steps.

Can you explain the 3 steps to an adult?

 Accepting when "no" really means "no"!

What can Beth do?

"No" means "no".

9
Learning to share

How do I learn to share things?

The **first** thing is to think about somebody else and not **yourself**.

If I share with you, will it make you happy?

Yes. I would be very happy.

Is he going to share back?

We can only hope he does.

Think of how **you** can play or work together on something.

It is much more **fun** with a friend.

I agree with that, so maybe sharing is a good thing after all.

Sharing

Learning to share

Let me tell you what happened to me.

I got a new game and my sister wanted to play.

I want to play, but you can have the first go because it will make us feel good to share.

I still want to go first. Even if it makes me selfish!

Give it to me now!

I need to talk to my Chimp to help it to be patient.

What does Joey say?

Learning to share

Learning to share

10

Doing what you have to do

Whether you like it or not!

Self-discipline

This means managing your Chimp!

Be very firm
with your Chimp!

Doing what you have to do

So Beth stopped her Chimp from thinking. **How do I learn to manage my Chimp?**

When your Chimp tells you not to do something or acts silly or makes excuses...

Ha! Making excuses is a special skill I have!

... that's the time to immediately tell it to STOP!

We can do it later when I feel like it.

Refuse to listen to your Chimp! It might NEVER feel like it!

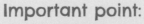

Important point:
The secret is to do things **immediately** and not let your Chimp think!

 We all have to look after ourselves.

 Yes I know. There are things we need to do that are good for us.

Going to bed.

 I don't want to go!

I know. Neither do I, but it is important to get my sleep.

Doing homework or other work.

 I need to get my work out of the way.

But it is so hard. I don't like to struggle.

It isn't nice, but moaning won't help. Let's just do it.

Having a shower or bath.

 It's time to have a bath. I don't want to be smelly.

No. I am just going to be stupid and mess about!

Bathroom

Doing what you have to do

Stop! Over to you to try it for yourself.

PRACTICE PAGE

Let's do a **role play!**

This means pretending.

Get an **adult** to help by asking you to do something.

Try this role play

First make your room a little messy and then pretend you are playing on a computer.

Then, I will come in and ask you to stop playing and tidy your room.

Pretend your Chimp is naughty and refuses.

Let your Chimp start being silly...

...THEN...

And do what needs to be done.
Tidy your room!

Important point:
It feels good to be sensible and make everyone happy.

 Doing what you have to do

Next!

How to manage your Chimp

Whether your Chimp likes it or not!

Here we go!

Sometimes you have to stop your Chimp
from speaking and behaving badly.

Here is an example of how my 3 steps work.

1st
STEP

My Chimp has taken over and is causing trouble so I tell it to **stop**.

 How to manage your Chimp

2nd STEP

I say **sorry** to whoever I have upset.

3rd STEP

I try to **do something nice** and put things right so that I am happy again.

Stop! It's time for YOU to try.

ACTIVITY PAGE

Try my **3 steps** to form the habit.

Work with an adult and have fun playing a game where your Chimp does something wrong and you need to say sorry.

So you could pretend to be naughty by being cheeky!

Practise using the 3 steps and see if you can do it well.

1st STEP

Be cheeky... but not too cheeky!

Shout out ... "My Chimp has taken over and is causing trouble - STOP IT!"

Be cheeky

Say STOP!

2nd STEP

Say "sorry" to whoever you have upset.

Say sorry

3rd STEP

Ask if there is anything you can do to put things right.

Give a big smile and be happy again.

Put it right

Smile

How to manage your Chimp

Carl is on his computer.

Write down the 3 steps to help Carl.

ACTIVITY PAGE

Stop! It's time for YOU to try.

Please help by writing down how I manage my Chimp, Fred.

Write your advice to Carl.

Write the words that go in the bubbles.

1st STEP

2nd STEP

3rd STEP

Psst... You might need to look back at Habit 8 for the answers.

154   How to manage your Chimp

ACTIVITY PAGE

The favourite thing that I have learnt is that I always have a choice.

I can either be a Chimp or I can be me.

You can help me by choosing what **YOU** would do in the following situations.

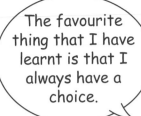

When we are outside being watched by other people and Banana-head gets naughty!...

... what should I do?

Just let my Chimp do what it likes.

Respect other people and tell my Chimp to behave.

Allow my Chimp to be a little bit naughty and then apologise.

Important point:

It is good to let your feelings out but it is important to do this in the right way and in the right place.

YOU decide which is the best way for me to manage my Chimp.

I am going to shout loudly!

I am going to explain that I am upset because I didn't do it.

I am never going to do anything ever again!

Important point:

Talk to an adult, but don't keep grumbling and complaining!

Which is the best way for my Chimp to react if I can't do something?

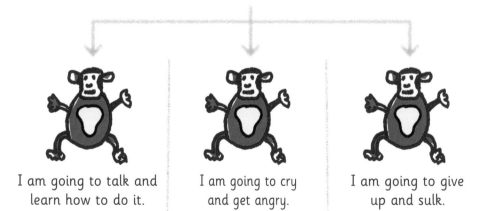

ACTIVITY PAGE

My Chimp usually hates to **lose** at anything.

So I have a chat with Banana-head before I play any game.

That way she will be prepared if we lose.

I do like to win, so a chat first might stop me from becoming embarrassing.

It's only a game and if we lose, it is not that important.

You're right, but I will still be disappointed.

I will be disappointed too but I am still going to enjoy the game.

Yes. We can still have fun and laugh, even if we lose.

How to manage your Chimp

Important point:

Your Chimp will feel better when it laughs at itself.

ACTIVITY PAGE

Stop! It's time for YOU to get busy.

I would like to know which **3 things** you have found helpful in this book.

1.

2.

3.

Also: Which habit will you practise every day?

_____

My habit.

Key points

First we learnt that we can think of the brain as 2 separate brains working alongside each other.

There is Our brain and our Chimp brain.

It is **NOT** a real Chimp brain!
We are just using the word "Chimp" for some parts of our brain that can act for us without our permission!

This is the part that we are calling the "Chimp".

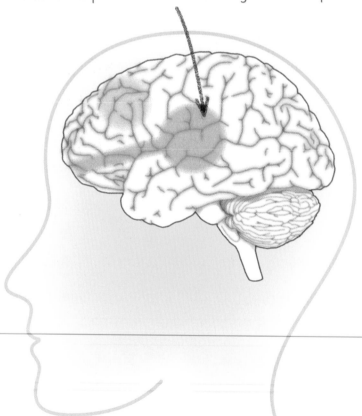

Key points

So we have...

Your brain	The Chimp brain

I am in charge of my brain and do what I want to do.

You

I am your Chimp brain and will take over if you don't manage me.

Your Chimp

We learnt to tell the difference between you and your Chimp.

Often what the Chimp wants is not what I want...

... and it might not be good!

Key points

Then we learnt that you always have a choice.

This is my favourite fact.

If you work with your brain then you will be sensible!

If you let your Chimp take over then it might make you look silly!

Your brain	The Chimp brain
I am happy.	I can be silly, worried or grumpy.

Important point:
You decide when you want to stop your Chimp from misbehaving.

TELL IT TO STOP!

Then apologise if it has caused any trouble!

Then we learnt about ten habits that could help to make you and other people happy.

Smiling. **1.**

Saying sorry. **2.**
It makes everyone feel better.

Being kind to someone. **3.**

Talking about your feelings. **4.**

Asking for help. **5.**

Showing good manners. 6.

Pleasing someone else by being polite.

Trying new things. 7.

Accepting when "no" 8.
really means "no"!

Learning to share. 9.

Doing what you have to do. 10.

Whether you like it or not!

We learnt that we need to practise the habits.

Try practising the ten habits by working with someone else, who is also doing them.

This could be a friend or even your parent!

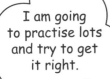

We learnt not to use our Chimp as an excuse to do hurtful or silly things.

 Key points

Managing your Chimp is like owning a pet dog.

You are responsible if your dog misbehaves.

You have to manage your dog.

It is up to **YOU** to manage your Chimp
and not use it as an excuse.

Your Chimp is part of you.

A VERY important point:
If your Chimp is not behaving, you can always ask for help from an adult.

Don't forget that your Chimp can ALSO be your best friend.

Important point:
Your Chimp can be your best friend.

Points to remember

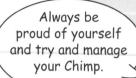

It isn't easy to manage your Chimp because it is **very strong.**

Important point:
Be happy with just being you. You are great just as you are!

Thank you for going on this journey with your team.

Key points

Also available:

Prof Steve Peters
CREATOR OF THE CHIMP MANAGEMENT MIND MODEL

Author of
The Chimp
Paradox
Over a million
copies sold

The
Silent
Guides

Understanding and developing
the mind throughout life

In **The Silent Guides**, Prof Steve Peters, author of the
bestselling **The Chimp Paradox**, explores the neuroscience and
psychological aspects of habit formation and related topics in
an easy to understand way. He then offers practical ideas and
thoughts for the reader to reflect on.